The
TRANSFORMATIVE
POWER of
GENEROSITY
TOWARD
GOD

The

TRANSFORMATIVE
POWER of
GENEROSITY
TOWARD
G O D

Bill English | Bible and
Business

ISBN: 979-8-218-23863-6

Bible and Business, Minneapolis, MN, USA
www.bibleandbusiness.com

To Kathy, who encouraged me to publish these sermons.

To Scott, for asking me to preach.

To Jesus Christ, for giving me the talent and opportunity to preach and write and without whom I would be lost forever.

Contents

Introduction

IN THE SPRING of 2021, I preached a four-part series[1] on generosity and stewardship at my local church (The Grove Church[2]) in Maple Grove, Minnesota. Providentially, I manuscripted those sermons, which means I wrote out my sermons word-for-word.

I firmly believe that generosity is the key to solving so many problems in our churches that it is difficult to overstate or exaggerate the importance of Christians becoming generous toward God. Becoming generous toward God can transform you in ways nothing else can.

I'm not offering a prosperity gospel—that's a theology I detest. But I am saying that when a person's money becomes available to God to further his kingdom, God does amazing things and that person's heart is fundamentally transformed in ways few other acts of discipleship can mimic.

I hope these sermons will bless and challenge you to become more generous toward God and that you'll experience real transformation and more spiritual health and wholeness as a result.

Bill English, July 2023
Maple Grove, Minnesota

---

1   The series was titled "A Generous People." You can find the series at mygrovechurch. org. https://thegrovechurchmn.subspla.sh/hvpchqw. Accessed June 21, 2023.

2   The Grove Church is a member of the Evangelical Free Church of America.

The
TRANSFORMATIVE
POWER of
GENEROSITY
TOWARD
G O D

PART I

Context of Stewardship

GOOD MORNING. I'M Bill English. I have been attending here for roughly 12 years, along with Kathy, my wife. For those visiting today, please understand that I am not on staff here, though I am seminary trained to be a pastor. Right now, I work in business in the turn-around field—the firm at which I'm a partner[3] takes businesses within days or hours of declaring bankruptcy, and we make them profitable again. In a good year, we'll save over a thousand jobs. Enough about me.

Last Fall, pastor Scott and I started to discuss stewardship in our church and what we could do to help others experience God's best for them in the area of stewardship and generosity. In early January, Scott asked if I would do a series on stewardship which was originally slated to be delivered after the *It's complicated* series. He had assigned me the last two Sundays in May and the first two in June to do this series.

So, let me start this series with the central idea that sums up all four Sundays in one sentence:

---

3   www.theplatinumgrp.com

Disciples of Jesus Christ are faithful to God in stewarding all He owns by disadvantaging themselves to advantage His kingdom.

Here is a "sneak preview" of these four Sundays:

Today: *The Context of Stewardship*. At a high level, I'll discuss covenants, faithfulness, and believing loyalty. We'll learn that covenants form the context for stewardship and generosity.

Next Sunday: *The Foundation of Stewardship*. Specifically, we'll look at ownership and entrustments in Matthew 25. We'll learn that God owns everything, and all we have are merely entrustments from God.

The Third Sunday: *The Life of Stewardship*. We'll consider a Biblical view of debt and saving and hoarding. We'll learn that the Bible discourages but does not prohibit debt. We'll also learn that hoarding is excessive saving.

The last Sunday: *The Heart of Stewardship*. We'll look at a Biblical view of generosity and giving within our covenant relationship with God.

I now fully believe that *financial generosity is the solution to so many problems in our church and society that it is difficult to overstate or exaggerate the importance of Christians becoming generous with their money and wealth.*

For the first part of this sermon, I'm relying heavily on two mentors.

One is Dr Michael Heiser's books and podcast called the Naked Bible podcast. Don't let the title fool you. He takes the inspired Word of God, strips away all the tradition and baggage we put on it, and expounds on the text. Listen to episode #350.

The other mentor is one of my seminary professors from whom I learned about covenants—Dr. McComiskey—who wrote the book *The Covenants of Promise*. I highly recommend the works of both men to you, though I will warn you, both are highly academic.

Covenants are Important

God has chosen to implement His redemptive plan through covenant relationships. And it is within the relationship of covenants that God asks us to steward all He has entrusted us.

Covenants are a rarely taught theology in most Evangelical churches. We tend to think of salvation as a personal relationship with Jesus Christ in which our sins are forgiven, and we try, as best we can, to live righteously before God. While this is all true, it lacks the context of covenants.

Many think the New Covenant did away with the Old Testament covenants. This isn't true. We'll learn this morning that the promises in the Old Testament covenants are in force today and will be throughout eternity. How we obey them changes with the New Covenant, but the New Covenant builds on the permanency of the promises God gave within the Old Testament covenants.

I will first look at three terms in the Old Testament; then, we will look at Deuteronomy 7 and other passages to put all this together.

Let's get started.

Old Testament Words

In the Old Testament, two words associated with each other express the concept of covenants.

The first word is *loving-kindness*. It's a straightforward phrase, and it means to be gracious and loving toward one who is in a covenant with you. But it's not a spontaneous emotion. It's not an uncontrolled love. It is a decisional, intentional love. Sometimes translated as steadfast love, loving-kindness is often associated with obligation and performance.

This is why loving kindness often appears with the Hebrew word for *faithfulness*. When they are used together—as they often are—we have the concepts of love and loyalty linked together. When we combine loving kindness with loyalty, we have a more accurate understanding of a covenant relationship. This is where the phrase *believing loyalty* comes from.

Finally, the word *covenant* appears often when these two words are associated in the text. So here is the trio of words: loving kindness, faithfulness and covenant.

God's Covenant with Abraham

Let's look at Abram and God's covenant with him in Genesis 12:1-3 (ESV):

> [1]Now the LORD said to Abram, "Go from your country and your kindred and your father's house to the land that I will show you. [2]And I will make of you a great nation, and I will bless you and make your name great, so that you will be a blessing. [3]I will bless those who bless you, and him who dishonors you I will curse, and in you all the families of the earth shall be blessed.

What did God promise Abram?
1. That he would make Abram's descendants into a great nation
2. He would bless Abram
3. His name would be great
4. Abram would have God's protection
5. Abram would be a blessing to others

Many believe this Abrahamic covenant to be unconditional with no strings attached. But this isn't the case. Covenants always come with stipulations. Covenants always contain benefits for obedience and penalties for disobedience.

For example, in Genesis 17, the Abrahamic covenant language is repeated but linked to Abram becoming circumcised.

Let's read Genesis 17.3-10 (ESV):

> And God said to him, [4]"Behold, my covenant is with you, and you shall be the father of a multitude of nations. [5]No longer shall your name be called Abram, but your name shall be Abraham, for I have made you the father of a multitude of nations. [6]I will make you exceedingly fruitful, and I will make you into nations,

and kings shall come from you. [7]And I will establish my covenant between me and you and your offspring after you throughout their generations for an everlasting covenant, to be God to you and to your offspring after you. [8]And I will give to you and to your offspring after you the land of your sojournings, all the land of Canaan, for an everlasting possession, and I will be their God." [9]And God said to Abraham, "As for you, you shall keep my covenant, you and your offspring after you throughout their generations. [10]This is my covenant, which you shall keep, between me and you and your offspring after you: Every male among you shall be circumcised.

In order for Abraham to enjoy the benefits of his covenant with God, he had to obey God by becoming circumcised.

So at the age of 99, Abram obeys, and all the males in his house, along with himself, were circumcised. When Abraham obeys, it is because he believes in the God who promised Him—he believes in the terms God promised in His covenant in Genesis 12 He believes that God will deliver.

Because Abraham believes, he obeys.

This is why *believing loyalty* is an accurate phrase that describes how the Bible views salvation in both Testaments. We believe, and because we believe, we want to obey. We demonstrate our loyalty to God through our obedience. Our obedience is our way of expressing our believing loyalty to God. Our hearts are transformed when we believe and want to obey God.

In this covenant relationship, we become His people, and He becomes our God. Believing loyalty means that we don't switch gods—we don't run to Allah, Moroni, Buddha, or some other god. We are loyal to believe in the God of the Bible. He is our God. We are His people. We are in a covenant with God.

Those who spurn God's love do not receive His loving-kindness or faithfulness. You must choose to enter into a covenant relationship with Him. You must believe that God can deliver on His promises and that no one else can. This is consistent across both testaments. Those who enter a covenant relationship with God believe that only He can save them from their sins. Only He can give them eternal life in his presence. Only God can do this. We believe this. And we become His people, and He becomes our God.

Now, there is a corporate aspect to covenants. When God says:

> "I will establish my covenant between me and you and I will be your God."

Here, God is speaking both corporately and individually. This is where it is important to understand that when we enter a covenant relationship with God, we are transferred from one kingdom to another, from one family to another, from one nation to another.

Let's look at Colossians 1.13 (NIV):

> For he has rescued us from the dominion of darkness and brought us into the kingdom of the Son, he love.

We become part of God's family—His Kingdom—when we enter a covenant relationship with Him. And in so doing, our heritage—our pedigree—our lineage goes back to Abraham. We become part of this great heritage God started with Abraham. We become part of the Covenant in Genesis 12.

Being brought into His kingdom means we enjoy the benefits of fellowship with each other. We also enjoy the loving kindness and loyalty of others who have covenanted with God.

We commit ourselves to others in our church because they have covenanted with God. We see ourselves as connected to a larger whole whom God is building to do significant ministry in our communities. And so we stick with each other. We do this because love and loyalty are foundational to a covenant relationship.

This is why Peter said in 1 Peter 4.8 (NIV): "love each other deeply, because love covers over a multitude of sins." When we love others, we're being loyal to them. And when we give love and loyalty to each other, we're living out our covenant relationship with each other and with God.

Now, we see all these elements in Deuteronomy 7:9-14 (ESV):

Know therefore that the Lord your God is God, the faithful God who keeps covenant and steadfast love with those who love him and keep his commandments, to a thousand generations, [10]and repays to their face those who hate him, by destroying them. He will not be slack with one who hates him. He will repay him to his face. [11]You shall therefore be careful to do the commandment and the statutes and the rules that I command you today. [12]"And because you listen to these rules and keep and do them, the Lord your God will keep with you the covenant and the steadfast love that he swore to your fathers. [13]He will love you, bless you, and multiply you. He will also bless the fruit of your womb and the fruit of your ground, your grain and your wine and your oil, the increase of your herds and the young of your flock, in the land that he swore to your fathers to give you. [14]You shall be blessed above all peoples.

In this passage, we see all the elements of a covenant. We see both love and loyalty. And we see our response of believing loyalty. We see God's loving-kindness—translated here as "steadfast love". And we see His faithfulness to us. We see loving kindness, faithfulness and covenant in the same passage.

In the New Testament, we find this connection of love, loyalty, and covenant in John 14.21, 23-24 (NIV) when Christ is speaking with His disciples in his Farwell Discourse as He is facing crucifixion:

Whoever has my commands and keeps them is the one who loves me. The one who loves me will be loved by my Father, and I too will love them and show myself to them…[23]Anyone who loves me will obey my teaching. My Father will love them, and we will come to them and make our home with them. [24]Anyone who does not love me will not obey my teaching. These words you hear are not my own; they belong to the Father who sent me.

Again, what do we see? Believing loyalty. We see that those who believe are also loyal. Those who believe obey God, and they obey because they believe.

So one of the big takeaways this morning is this:

> When we enter into a personal relationship with Christ, it's not a relationship in which we enjoy a full suite of fire-saving benefits where obedience to God is optional.

Instead, when we enter into a personal relationship with God, *we enter into a covenant relationship in which we obey because we believe.* We enter into a covenant relationship in which we pledge to be faithful to Him, knowing He is faithful to us. It is a two-way street. It is a covenant. Belief must precede behavior. This is not optional. You can't earn your salvation. You must believe by faith, and then obedience will follow.

One note of encouragement here:

That which cannot be gained through performance cannot be lost through lack of performance. We don't gain salvation through our performance because performance follows belief. But we also don't lose our salvation through lack of performance. The basis of our covenant with God is focused on believing loyalty to God. We don't switch Gods. But we also keep the right order in mind: we believe first, then we obey. This is essential and is consistent in both testaments. Salvation comes through genuine belief. You don't obey to believe. You believe, then you obey.

In the Old Testament, believing loyalty was evidenced by keeping the law. You believed, so you obeyed the law.

But over the years, the old testament law devolved into a system of duty where outward obedience became all that mattered. Believing loyalty didn't matter. They put the cart before the horse.

So, when Christ came, He ushered in a new covenant initially outlined in the books of Isaiah, Jeremiah and Ezekiel.

So, let's look more closely at this New Covenant.

Let's read Jeremiah 31.31,33 (NIV):

³¹The days are coming," declares the Lord, "when I will make a new covenant with the people of Israel and with the people of Judah…³³…"I will put my law in their minds and write it on their hearts. I will be their God, and they will be my people.

The core of this new covenant is that God would write his law into our hearts—obedience would be administered not through an outward set of laws and rules which focused on behavioral change but through an inward change in our hearts such that we would want to do what God has commanded. We would want to be faithful to God.

Did you catch what God would do? He would write his law in our minds and on our hearts.

When God writes His laws on our hearts, He is transforming our hearts to love what He loves and hates what He hates. That which brings God joy will bring us joy. That which brings God sorrow will bring us sorrow as well. God gives us the love for Him, which we need to be faithful to Him in our covenant with Him.

As part of this new covenant, God places His Spirit within us.

Let's read Ezekiel 36.25-28 (ESV):

²⁵I will sprinkle clean water on you, and you shall be clean from all your uncleannesses, and from all your idols I will cleanse you. ²⁶And I will give you a new heart, and a new spirit I will put within you. And I will remove the heart of stone from your flesh and give you a heart of flesh. ²⁷And I will put my Spirit within you, and cause you to walk in my statutes and be careful to obey my rules. ²⁸You shall dwell in the land that I gave to your fathers, and you shall be my people, and I will be your God.

When God puts His Spirit within us, He will "move us"—*cause us*—to follow His decrees and laws.

That's inner transformation—not outward obedience to a set of rules. Jeremiah and Ezekiel tell us that God will transform us from the inside out in the new covenant.

But similar to how we must enter into a covenant with God, we must choose to allow God to transform us. We can resist the Spirit's work within us. We can resist God writing His laws in our minds and hearts. We're not passive. We're not robots. God doesn't program us to make us act a certain way. No. We believe, then we obey, and when we obey, we cooperate with God and allow Him to transform how we think and what we love.

And I think this is how lukewarm Christians come to be—they don't let God finish His work in them. They embrace the parts of Christianity that they like and reject the parts they don't like. The parts that are inconvenient or ask for sacrifice—the parts we must believe in despite our experiences—the parts that touch their money and wealth—well—they don't like that. So they pick and choose which parts they'll accept.

For example, next Sunday, I'll teach that God owns everything, including all your money. It's not like God gets 10%, and you get 90%. That's not what the Bible teaches. We merely steward what He owns. This means He gets to tell us how to spend it. In other words, we spend the money in our bank accounts at His discretion, not ours. Some will not like this teaching. Their challenge will be this: "will I let God write that part of His law into my mind and heart?" Will I have a hard heart toward God or a soft heart toward Him?

These lukewarm Christians are trying to gain the benefits of a covenant relationship with God while also holding tight to the things of this world. They love the things of this world while trying to love God. If they are honest, they have an ongoing conflict within themselves about their affections.

You see, at the core of this series is your heart. Giving is always a heart issue. It is never about capacity or ability.

Show me someone who doesn't give to God's work, and I'll show you someone who loves the things of this earth and whose heart is not fully with God. God still needs to write his laws into the heart and mind of that person.

If this is you, then know this: in the long run, you'll either abandon your relationship with God or let go of your love for the things of this world. You'll eventually be forced to choose. And know this also—eventually, God rejects those who are lukewarm. So, I urge you to let God fully write His law into your mind and heart so that you fully embrace the New Covenant.

What have we learned this morning?

First, we have learned that a personal relationship with God is a covenant relationship in which love and loyalty are combined. We have also learned that believing loyalty is visceral to maintaining our covenant relationship with God.

Secondly, we have learned that if we enter the new covenant fully, we must allow God to fully write His law into our minds and hearts—to transform how we think and love. You cannot have all of what God wants to give you while still loving the things of this world. You cannot have God's best and still hang onto the things you love dearly.

Disciples of Jesus Christ are faithful to God in stewarding all He owns by disadvantaging themselves to advantage His kingdom.

As we wrap up this morning, I have one question and one invitation.

First, if you're a Christian—if you claim to be a Disciple of Jesus Christ—then my question for you this morning is this: Will you pledge yourself to God and let him write His laws into your mind and heart? Will you demonstrate believing loyalty by allowing God to write his laws on your mind and in your heart?

My invitation is for those who don't know if they have entered into a covenant relationship with God. If you're listening this morning, and you're sensing you don't have a personal, covenant relationship with God, then my invitation is to invite Him into your heart and pledge yourself to God this morning.

If you have made a decision to enter into a covenant relationship with Christ, be sure to tell someone today. I'll be here—you can always talk with me or our prayer team who will be up here after the service.

And if you don't have a church home, we would love to get you connected here at the Grove and see how we can help you in your journey with God. Stop by the Connect Center or speak with someone today. With God, every day can be a fresh start—a new beginning. I hope today is a new beginning for you.

PART II:

Foundation of Stewardship

G OOD MORNING. WE'RE on the 2nd Sunday of a four-part series
focused on stewardship and generosity.

The overriding theme we're working with in this series is this:

**Disciples of Jesus Christ are faithful to God in stewarding
all He owns by disadvantaging themselves to advantage
His kingdom.**

Last week, we considered the Context of Stewardship. We learned that our
covenant relationship with God is the context in which Christian stewardship
can thrive.

We learned that a covenant is a relationship characterized by loving kindness and loyalty—love and loyalty. We learned that covenants have both
individual and corporate aspects to them. We learned that a personal relationship with God is a covenantal relationship. We saw how our covenant
relationship with God leads us to covenant relationships with each other. We
learned that salvation is believing loyalty to God. We were also encouraged

to learn that since we can't earn our salvation through our performance, we cannot lose our salvation through lack of performance.

We learned that the new covenant enables us to be faithful to God because God transforms us from the inside out by writing His law into our minds and hearts. But we also noted how we could short-circuit His transforming work by resisting His efforts to write His law into our minds and hearts.

And we faced a penetrating question last week: "Will you participate in the new covenant by allowing God to write His laws fully into your mind and heart?"

Today, we're going to look at the Foundation of Stewardship. We'll learn five foundational truths upon which Christian stewardship is based.

So let's open our Bibles to Matthew 25.14 (NIV). We will look at the parable of the talents and learn about the five Foundations of Stewardship. Let's read this together.

> [14]"Again, it will be like a man going on a journey, who called his servants and entrusted his wealth to them. [15]To one he gave five bags of gold, to another two bags, and to another one bag, each according to his ability. Then he went on his journey. [16]The man who had received five bags of gold went at once and put his money to work and gained five bags more. [17]So also, the one with two bags of gold gained two more. [18]But the man who had received one bag went off, dug a hole in the ground and hid his master's money. [19]"After a long time the master of those servants returned and settled accounts with them. [20]The man who had received five bags of gold brought the other five. 'Master,' he said, 'you entrusted me with five bags of gold. See, I have gained five more.' [21]"His master replied, 'Well done, good and faithful servant! You have been faithful with a few things; I will put you in charge of many things. Come and share your master's happiness!' [22]"The man with two bags of gold also came. 'Master,' he said, 'you entrusted me with two bags of gold; see, I have gained two more.' [23]"His master replied, 'Well done, good and faithful servant! You have been faithful with a few things;

I will put you in charge of many things. Come and share your master's happiness!' ²⁴"Then the man who had received one bag of gold came. 'Master,' he said, 'I knew that you are a hard man, harvesting where you have not sown and gathering where you have not scattered seed. ²⁵So I was afraid and went out and hid your gold in the ground. See, here is what belongs to you.' ²⁶"His master replied, 'You wicked, lazy servant! So you knew that I harvest where I have not sown and gather where I have not scattered seed? ²⁷Well then, you should have put my money on deposit with the bankers, so that when I returned I would have received it back with interest. ²⁸"'So take the bag of gold from him and give it to the one who has ten bags. ²⁹For whoever has will be given more, and they will have an abundance. Whoever does not have, even what they have will be taken from them. ³⁰And throw that worthless servant outside, into the darkness, where there will be weeping and gnashing of teeth.'

We need to set the context just a bit. Some have preached that this passage refers mainly to spiritual riches in which the servants create spiritual returns on their work.

But when you read this in the Greek, the keywords used are economic and monetary words. For example, the Greek word we translate, "bags of gold", refers to a unit of weight and measurement in the coinage of money. The sense of the word is "a large monetary measurement." In other words, a certain weight of a valuable metal. In addition, when the master says that the wicked servant should have earned interest on his one bag of gold, the Greek word for "interest" is monetary. It means "the profits arising from lending money".

The passage doesn't make sense if we're talking only about spiritual profits. You can't take spiritual talents and put them in a bank. You can't take a spiritual gift and somehow double your gifting in the marketplace. Instead, it is right to see this parable referring to real economic wealth and real monetary profit.

We should also note that this parable assumes that creating profits is an act of discipleship. Profits are seen as good. Profits are not attacked as inherently being evil in this parable.

What are the foundational truths we can learn about stewardship from this parable?

Foundational Truth #1: God Owns Everything.

We see this in the first part of the parable:

> [14]Again, it will be like a man going on a journey, who called his servants and entrusted his wealth to them. [15]To one he gave five bags of gold, to another two bags, and to another one bag, each according to his ability.

There is no doubt that the Master owns the money. His servants used His money to generate real wealth. The servants didn't go to the bank and invest their own money. They used the Master's money to create profit.

This idea that God owns everything is also clearly stated in other passages in the Bible.

Let's read Psalm 50.9-12 (NIV):

> I have no need of a bull from your stall or of goats from your pens, for every animal of the forest is mine, and the cattle on a thousand hills. I know every bird in the mountains, and the insects in the fields are mine. If I were hungry, I would not tell you, for the world is mine, and all that is in it.

Psalm 24.1 (NIV) says:

> The earth is the Lord's and everything in it, the world, and all who live in it.

If God owns everything, then it stands to reason that He owns your business, money, and wealth. He owns your house, your cars, your cabin, your season tickets, your investments and so forth. We may own things in the American, legal sense. But in God's economy, He owns it all.

Christianity has some paradoxes. (By the way, a paradox is a seemingly self-contradictory statement that proves to be well founded and true when investigated.) We gain by losing. We become strong when we become weak. We become elevated through humility. The last shall be first.

God's ownership of everything is somewhat of a paradox. Our culture values ownership and encourages us to claim ownership of everything we can. It's not like we need encouragement. You'll see little children do this—they don't need to be taught to claim ownership over a toy. They do it naturally. And we think that gaining ownership and control over things in our environment will give us the good life. We'll find happiness. We'll find financial security. We'll find what we're looking for.

But how we experience God's best for us is an apparent paradox: we release our ownership of what we have to God, and in exchange, we find a real life of joy and happiness. We gain financial security by giving our money away. We'll find peace by trusting in God for our financial future rather than trusting in our investments. We'll be more fulfilled when we buy less and give away more. We'll be salt and light by helping others who are hurting. And our church will be stronger when we're more generous.

America says that the good life is to be the master of your domain. But God says the great life is to be a steward in God's domain.

So, to reiterate, the first foundation of all Christian Stewardship is this: **God Owns Everything.**

Foundational Truth #2: God entrusts to us some of what He owns.

Because God owns everything, He has the authority and right to entrust the care and feeding of what He owns to anyone He chooses.

As a result, biblical stewardship views everything we have as an entrustment from God because God owns everything we have. Let's look at the parable again—especially verse 15:

"To one he gave five bags of gold, to another two bags, and to another one bag, each according to his ability."

The act of giving while maintaining ownership is the classic definition of entrusting. The master gave bags of gold to the servants, but he never relinquished his ownership of that gold.

Becoming a servant—a steward—of what God owns goes against our natural tendencies. Our culture pushes us to take charge and pick ourselves up by our bootstraps. Don't let others run your life. Follow your heart. Do what you think is right. Don't let anyone tell you how you should live. And when we're in charge, that's living the good life.

But God says we can have a great life by becoming a steward. We can finally rest in God's sovereignty. We no longer need to be burdened and work ourselves until weary. We come to God, and He lifts those burdens. This is how we find the great life—we become a steward. And we steward well all that He has entrusted to us.

And it's not just material goods which are entrusted to us.

Let's look at 1 Thessalonians 2.4 (NIV):

> On the contrary, we speak as those approved by God to be entrusted with the Gospel.

Let's not forget that God owns the Gospel too. This is why, when He decides to call people to preach or share the good news of the Gospel, He is entrusting that to them. Now, entrustment of the preaching and sharing of the Gospel is a big deal. You'll recall Christ gave us the Great Commission in Matthew 28—to go into all the world and make disciples, teaching them to obey everything God has commanded. That is a huge entrustment to the church. God owns His commands. And he entrusts them to us to teach to others.

Spreading the Gospel and making disciples are highly important in God's economy. In Luke 16.10-12 (NIV), these activities are called "true riches" and are compared to worldly wealth:

> [10]Whoever can be trusted with very little can also be trusted with much, and whoever is dishonest with very little will also be dishonest with much. [11]So if you have not been trustworthy in handling worldly wealth, who will trust you with true riches?

[12]And if you have not been trustworthy with someone else's property, who will give you property of your own?

The comparison Christ is making is between worldly wealth and true riches. The contrast is between that which is temporal and that which is eternal. "Worldly wealth" is temporal—it is the small stuff. The true riches of spreading the Gospel and discipleship are the permanent, abiding, hence "true" riches.

The point Christ makes is that if you're not trustworthy in how you manage "worldly wealth"—the temporal stuff—the small stuff—then how does God know you'll be faithful if He entrusts to you the big stuff—true riches—of sharing the Gospel and making disciples? To boil this down to common English, the comparison is this: If you're not living a life dedicated to God, why would God give you opportunities to lead others to Christ? If you're not managing well the monetary wealth God has entrusted you, then he won't entrust you the opportunity to lead others to Christ and then disciple them. He's not going to take that chance.

We must first prove ourselves faithful in the small stuff—worldly riches—before He'll consider giving us the more important, eternal and permanent work called "true riches."

This is the reason most churches are not "soul-winning" churches. They are not faithful in the small stuff. They are not generous toward God. So they are unable to be faithful in the big stuff. God doesn't let them have that opportunity.

This ties together our money management and generosity to our maturity in Christ. If you're not managing your money the way God would have you manage it—if you've not given God control of all your money and wealth—then you're not being faithful to Him with the small stuff—the worldly wealthy—and God cannot entrust to you the true riches of sharing the Gospel and making disciples.

I've come to believe that most Christians rarely sense God's presence or witness effectively or cannot be mighty in prayer or experience a deep and abiding presence with God because they have not been faithful in the small stuff. They haven't been faithful to God with their money, so God can't entrust them with true riches.

If you're not generous toward God, you're likely not feeling or sensing God's presence. God won't entrust true riches to you until you have surrendered your chequebook, investments, and money to Him. You will only progress so far in your walk with God until you see yourself as a steward instead of an owner. You and I will never draw intimately close to God without first surrendering ownership of our wealth to Him.

Foundational Truth #3: God Gives Entrustments to Us Based on the Abilities He Has Given to Us

Let's look at the phrase "according to his ability."

> "To one he gave five bags of gold, to another two bags, and to another one bag, each according to his ability."

God gives us different abilities. Most of us create wealth by working for others. But some create wealth by employing others. We each have been given abilities in this area. One ability is not more important than another.

America says that to have a good life, you must believe in yourself and work hard to get all you can. America says you have no idea of the power of your own abilities. So, strive hard to win. Accomplish all you can. And when you do, you will have found the good life.

Now look, I understand that if we get some confidence in ourselves and push ourselves, we can usually accomplish more than we thought we could.

But God says you and I will find a great life by believing in Him and letting His Spirit energize us to do what He asks us to do. The great life is found in being faithful to God within our covenant relationship. God gives us enough abilities to accomplish everything He calls us to do. And doing what God wants us to do is maximizing our abilities. America tells us to push ourselves until we have found the outer limits of our abilities. God gives us just the right mix and amount of abilities to fulfil His call on our lives. The great life is not found in discovering all that I can do but in discovering all that God has called me to do.

If we are talented, the Lord created us that way. If we are smart, it is because God gave us our intelligence. If we are creative—that's from God too. If we have significant opportunities to create wealth, the Lord has positioned us to do so. If we have been given significant wealth through inheritance, the Lord has been generous to us. If we have a new product idea for a better mouse trap, the Lord has given it to us. We learn to enjoy and celebrate our differences because, within our covenant relationships with God and each other, we understand that we're building God's kingdom on this earth and preparing to reign with Him in eternity. And this collective effort requires different abilities.

So, we've learned so far that 1) God owns everything and 2) all that we have are entrustments from Him, and 3) He gives entrustments to us based on the abilities He gave us.

But there's more.

Foundational Truth #4: Stewards Know Their Master Well

Faithfully stewarding entrustments means we must know the Master's heart—they know Him well.

The relationship of the first two servants with the master was substantively different from that of the third servant. The single variable between the first two servants and the third was their view of the master, which was derived from the varying quality of their relationship with the master.

Said a different way, the two good servants had a healthy relationship with the master, and the third did not.

We see this in how the third servant responded to the Master:

> "[24]I knew that you are a hard man, harvesting where you have not sown and gathering where you have not scattered seed. [25]So I was afraid…"

But the Master wasn't a hard man, oppressing his employees or taking wealth from others unfairly. He wasn't a difficult man to work for.

Instead, this was an excuse the wicked servant offered in the hopes of covering up his laziness. Lazy people always blame others for their laziness.

> [26]His master replied, 'You wicked, lazy servant! So you knew that I harvest where I have not sown and gather where I have not scattered seed? [27]Well then, you should have put my money on deposit with the bankers, so that when I returned I would have received it back with interest.

The wicked servant was so lazy that he didn't even try to go to the bank and earn interest on the money, which would have been easy to do. The wicked servant was just plain lazy. Had he made an effort to get to know the master, he would have known what to do.

The application here is obvious: lazy Christians don't pursue God and are not faithful stewards. They don't make even minimal efforts to know Him. As a result, they develop wrong ideas and impressions of who He is. And Satan uses their laziness to slowly but surely, entice them to drift away from Him. Over time, lazy Christians can switch gods and thus become unfaithful and leave their covenant relationship with Him.

Pursuing God is a lost discipline in today's evangelical circles. We are Bible-studied to death, but most of what we learn doesn't translate into effective worship, prayer, witnessing, or generosity. We often portray God as a cosmic bellhop whose main interest is serving us. But covenant relationships are a two-way street. God has already taken the initiative to connect with us. We need to take the initiative to connect with Him.

People who live great lives do so because they intentionally draw close to God's heart. They know God well because they take the time to know Him. They love the Lord and grow increasingly in their love for Him. They avoid evil because they have set their heart on seeking God's face. Faithful stewards know that God rewards those who diligently seek Him. They look to the Lord in times of trouble and depend on His strength. They understand His spiritual protection, which comes from walking closely with Him. They ask Him what to do in myriad situations. They know and listen to His voice. They confess their sins regularly, and they delight in learning His law. They develop an intuitive sense of God's desires in a given situation, even if they can't point to chapter and verse. When they pray, you can sense the anointing of God resting on them. They love the fellowship of other Christians. Others are drawn to the Lord because of their walk with God. They enjoy the sweetness of His presence, the beauty of His holiness, the discernment of the Holy Spirit, the power of His protection, and the leading of His voice. They feel His pleasure.

And there is ***nothing*** in this world they would trade for these true riches. They have traded the American good life for the great one we can find only in our covenant relationship with God. And when you meet these people, you'll find they are generous toward God. To a person. Every time.

Before we go on, I want to encourage you here. If you set yourself to pursue the heart of God, then give it time. I think you'll find He will give you His heart in proportion to how you allow Him to transform your heart. That's my experience. God shows Himself to me as I allow Him to change me. And when I resist, He backs off. Then I re-engage, and we reconnect.

There is nuance here. And it is intimate. All of this takes time, and the more you connect with God, the less concerned you'll be about the time or the effort. Connecting with God is so worth it! You'll be the man who sold everything he had to buy the pearl. So be encouraged. Living close to God is the great life that God offers us. To know His heart…what a joy!

Foundational Truth #5: If We Are Faithful to God, We will Reign With Him Throughout Eternity

Let's look at the parable one more time:

> [23]"Well done, good and faithful servant! You have been faithful with a few things; I will put you in charge of many things. Come and share your master's happiness!"

The faithful servants—what was their reward? It was two things:
1. They were put in charge of much more valuable things than money
2. They were given more of the Master's presence

This theme in the Bible states, essentially, that if we are faithful to God—love and loyalty—until we die, part of our reward will be to reign with Him in eternity. And we will do so in His presence, enjoying Him and reigning over what He will entrust us.

This thrust of reigning with Him is given to us in 2 Timothy as well: 2 Timothy 2.11-12 (ESV):

> [11]If we died with him, we will also live with him; [12]if we endure, we will also reign with him

Hence, what we do on this earth, both in activity and drawing close to God, is preparatory for reigning with Him in eternity. For a disciple of Jesus Christ, our primary preparation on this earth is not to have a fulfilling career—as important as that is in many instances. It is, instead, to prepare to reign with Christ in eternity by being faithful to Him and learning to enjoy His presence.

If you want God's great life, adopt an eternal perspective on everything you do. When we learn to hear His voice and follow His leading, we're preparing to reign with Him. We're preparing to reign with Him when we draw close to Him. We're preparing to reign with Him when we represent Him well to a lost and broken world. Our perspectives of this life will change when we connect our temporal world to our eternal time with Him. The things of this world will grow strangely dim in the light of His glory and grace. This is the great life. And nothing this world offers can compare to it.

Today, we have learned that God owns everything. Therefore, everything we have is an entrustment from Him. But to steward what He has entrusted to us well, we need to know and understand His heart, agenda, and intentions for that which He owns.

We've also learned that God gives us the ability to create wealth. And if we remain faithful in our covenant with Him, then our reward is more of His presence and reigning over greater entrustments in eternity. What we do on this earth is preparatory for how we will spend eternity with Christ.

Last week, our stewardship question was this: Will you allow God to write His laws fully into your mind and heart?

Our Stewardship Question this week is this:

Will you be a faithful steward who properly cares for God's entrustments and takes the time and effort to know Him intimately?

Will you say "yes" to God this morning?

Disciples of Jesus Christ are faithful to God in stewarding all He owns by disadvantaging themselves to advantage His kingdom.

Let's pray.

PART III

Life of Stewardship

GOOD MORNING. WE'RE on the 3rd Sunday of a four-part series on Christian stewardship.

The central idea that we're working with is this:

Disciples of Jesus Christ are faithful to God in stewarding all He owns by disadvantaging themselves to advantage His kingdom.

On the first Sunday, we looked at the Context for Stewardship. We learned that the context for stewardship is our covenant relationship with God.

We learned that a personal relationship with God is a covenantal relationship based on loving loyalty.

We saw how the new covenant enables us to be faithful to God because God transforms us by writing His law into our minds and hearts. Instead of administrating obedience through outward conformity to law, God gives us a new nature in which we want to obey Him.

But we also noted how we could short-circuit His transforming work by resisting His efforts to write His law into our minds and hearts.

And we faced this question: "Will you participate in the new covenant by allowing God to write His laws fully into your mind and heart?"

Last week, we looked at the Foundation of Stewardship by diving into the parable of the bags of gold from Matthew 25.

We learned about ownership and entrustments. We learned that God owns everything, and everything we have is a matrix of entrustments from God to be stewarded by us to further God's Kingdom. And these entrustments are given to us according to the abilities God has given us.

We also learned that as stewards, we need to draw close to the heart of God if we're going to manage well what God has entrusted to us.

And finally, we learned that our present stewardship of God's entrustment to us prepares us to reign with God in eternity. No matter what we're doing here on earth, it is preparatory for our stewardship role of reigning with Him.

We faced an important question: "Will you be a faithful steward who properly cares for God's entrustments and takes the time and effort to know Him intimately?"

In other words, will you give up being an owner and become a steward?

Today, we're going to look at the Life of Stewardship. We're going to consider three areas which, it seems to me, must be managed well if we're going to become generous toward God:

- Debt
- Saving
- Hoarding

Until we have come into alignment with His instructions in these three areas, I doubt we'll be able to become generous toward God.

So let's get started.

A Biblical View of Debt

Debt has two sides: lending and borrowing.

Let's start by considering Deuteronomy 15.6 (NIV) and 28.12 (NIV):

15:6: For the Lord your God will bless you as he has promised, and you will lend to many nations but will borrow from none

28:12: The LORD will open the heavens, the storehouse of his bounty, to send rain on your land in season and to bless all the work of your hands. You will lend to many nations but will borrow from none.

According to these scriptures, faithfully obeying God's commandments results in being blessed, giving you the ability to lend, and having little need to borrow. The blessing doesn't mean you'll be financially rich, but you will be able to live today on the fruit of today's labors. You won't be living today on tomorrow's income.

R.C. Sproul Jr. has written one of the best books I've ever read on economics: *Biblical Economics: A Commonsense Guide to Our Daily Bread.*[4] He wrote:

"Debt, whether you are buying hamburgers, books, CDs, or a car, is the practice of consuming today the fruit of tomorrow's labor. It is consuming more than you produce…If you consume today what you will produce tomorrow, what will you consume tomorrow?

When we perpetually live consuming tomorrow's wealth today, we place ourselves into a never-ending cycle of "feeding the beast"—working to pay off debt while accumulating more debt for the future.

As a country, we have already spent decades of future productivity on ourselves through our national and state debts. So, at the personal level, we take on debt thinking it's not a big deal. And for some here today, our lifestyles are built largely on debt. We go into debt for homes, cars, cabins, furniture, boats, season tickets, etc. We think we're OK as long as we can make the payments. Our culture has taught us to take on debt—as long as you can afford the payments, then you're managing your money well.

Sometimes, debt is thrust upon us through medical bills, unforeseen accidents, business failure, etc.

---

4   RC Sproule Jr. (2010) *Biblical Economics: A Common Sense Guide to Our Daily Bread.* White hall, WV: Tolle Lege Press. Kindle edition. Location 1285.

Sustained, high debt levels have negative consequences. For example, missing one or two paychecks can put some forever behind, unable to get caught up on their payments.

High debt leads to high stress. Sustained stress, in turn, can cause physical problems that may persist for long periods, degrading the quality of our lives.

Debt harms our marriages too. In a study of more than 4500 married couples, researchers saw that couples who took on more debt over time became more likely to split up. Couples with higher debt fought more about money and reported lower marital satisfaction.

Debt harms our church too. Many Christians are in bondage to debt and are significantly hindered in their service and generosity to the Lord because of their debt. God can't call them to the mission field or any full-time vocational ministry, nor can He call them to meet the needs of their next-door neighbor because they are so laden with debt. In other words, high debt limits our productivity for the Lord.

I believe debt is one reason over half of our church body never gives any money—not even $1—during any 12-month period.[5] Many cannot give simply because their debt has a claim on their income for years to come. This debt harms our church, our witness for Christ, and our effectiveness for the Kingdom.

Debt divides our allegiances. Let's look at Proverbs 22.7 (NIV):

The rich rule over the poor and the borrower is slave to the lender.

When we take on debt, a portion of our labor is now serving the interests of another.

When our allegiances are divided, we're not fully available to God. This division of allegiances is why many mission organizations require those going to the mission field to be completely free of any debt. Debt divides our loyalties. Debt can hinder our effectiveness for God.

For some listening to my sermon this morning, your challenge in becoming generous toward God is less about your willingness to give and more about long-term, structural debt: how will you become generous toward Him when you can barely make your monthly payments now?

---

5   This is true in most Evangelical churches; over half of those who attend an Evangelical church never give even $1 to that church in any given 12 month period.

If you are in debt, then what should you do?

1. **Stop the bleeding.** Stop creating more debt. Make whatever lifestyle choices you must make to live on the fruit of today's labors. In this same vein, if you have assets you can sell to help pay off your debt, ask God if you should do this.

2. **Work with a financial planner** to build a long-term plan to pay off your debt. Find a planner who is willing to work with you on the debt side so that in the future, you might be able to work with them on the investment side. Most won't do this, but a few will.

3. **Slowly build an emergency fund** to cover unexpected expenses. It may be that much of your debt has come from unexpected expenses. Good stewardship would indicate that we should plan for the unexpected.

4. **Start giving consistently to God**—even if it is just a $1 week. As you pay off debts and your cash flow improves, increase the amounts you give God.

The hard part here will be to stop using debt to prop up a standard of living above where we should be. In some situations, debt allows us to gratify our desires instantly. The structural change is submitting to God, who may ask us to live with prolonged, delayed gratification to stay out of debt and be more available for ministry.

So this begs the question: when should we take on debt? The Bible doesn't explicitly instruct us in this question, so I'll offer some ideas. This is Bill, not Bible. But I think I have God's mind on this: we take on debt only when we're led to do so by God.

This suggestion comes from the general notion that when we walk in God's will, we hear His voice and follow Him. If we take on debt when He doesn't want us to do so, we get outside His will, provision, and protection. But when we stay inside His will, we enjoy the blessings of His provision and protection. So, it seems wise to take on debt only when God tells us to do so.

To sum up, here is the core, Biblical principle for assuming debt:

When we borrow, our allegiances become divided between God and our lender. So don't borrow unless God leads you to do so.

A Biblical View of Saving

On the opposite end of borrowing and consuming the fruit of tomorrow's labor today is saving for future expenses. Saving sets aside some of the fruit of today's labor to be consumed tomorrow.

Believe it or not, the Bible does speak to saving. So the logical question is this: what does the Bible say about saving for the future? Well, the Bible emphasizes two main reasons to save:

1. To pay for future expenses
2. To give to others who are in need

Let's look at paying for future expenses by reading about Joseph in Genesis 41.46-49 (NIV):

> [46]Joseph was thirty years old when he entered the service of Pharaoh king of Egypt. And Joseph went out from Pharaoh's presence and traveled throughout Egypt. [47]During the seven years of abundance the land produced plentifully. [48]Joseph collected all the food produced in those seven years of abundance in Egypt and stored it in the cities. In each city he put the food grown in the fields surrounding it. [49]Joseph stored up huge quantities of grain, like the sand of the sea; it was so much that he stopped keeping records because it was beyond measure.

Joseph's preparation for famine in Egypt is a prime example of seeing one's need for money and resources and saving for the future out of one's abundance in the present. Because the king trusted Joseph, he knew the lack of grain in the future would be severe, so the king allowed Joseph to save up grain out of the seven-year abundance.

The principle to learn here is that *our present savings should be roughly equivalent to our future needs*. Biblical saving attempts to save for future needs out of present abundance.

Secondly, saving in the present to give in the future is also encouraged and illustrated in 1 Corinthians 16.1-2 (NIV):

¹Now about the collection for the Lord's people: Do what I told the Galatian churches to do. ²On the first day of every week, each one of you should set aside a sum of money in keeping with your income, saving it up, so that when I come no collections will have to be made.

The Jerusalem church oversaw the churches that Paul founded. Yet we have no scriptural evidence that the Jerusalem church levied taxes on Gentile Christians, unlike the Jerusalem priests who compelled the Jews in Israel and in dispersion to pay the annual temple tax.

Rather, Paul taught Gentile believers that they should joyfully share material blessings with the Jewish Christians in Jerusalem because the Jerusalem saints had shared with them spiritual blessings. Paul wanted them to be cheerful givers who, without reluctance or compulsion, generously gave their gifts to support people experiencing poverty.

Since they didn't have a banking system with electronic transfer capabilities, physical money had to be carried from point A to point B. So Paul was asking the gentile believers in Corinth and other cities to save up so that they could give to their brothers in Jerusalem who were in desperate need.

The principle here is this: *It is honoring to God to set aside a portion of your wealth with the express intention of giving it away.* So, it seems to me that the thrust of what pleases God is for us to structure our lives so that after reasonably saving for the future, we give the balance of our wealth away.

I can't point to a single chapter and verse which says this, but when we align passages that illustrate saving with passages that talk about meeting the needs of our brothers, I think this notion accurately represents the mind of God. We save for the future to cover future expenses during those times when we're not able to generate wealth like we can today. Then we give the rest of our wealth away.

The huge benefit of giving the rest of our wealth away is that it will cause us to remain dependent on God. This notion of financial security—financial independence—***is lethal to the cause of Christ***. God always provides for our needs, but He will not provide enough for us to become independent from Him.

At this point, some may say, "Wait a minute—what about providing an inheritance for our children? Are you saying leaving an inheritance for our children or grandchildren is wrong?"

Not at all. The Bible speaks positively about leaving an inheritance for your children and grandchildren. So while I don't have time to give this topic the attention it deserves, bear in mind there is a basic principle that scholars and Pastors use to interpret the Bible—which I think is relevant here: Emphasize what the Bible emphasizes and don't emphasize that which the Bible doesn't emphasize.

For example, when we combine the frequency of how often the Greek and Hebrew words for giving, gold, silver, wealth, money, generosity, stewardship, and so forth appear in the Bible, you'll find this larger topic of money and wealth is mentioned over 1000 times in the Bible. Now, consider that there are only 1189 chapters in the Bible. This means that, on average, the Bible talks about money and wealth nearly once per chapter in the Bible.

By the same token, when it comes to giving to others who have a present need vs. leaving an inheritance of wealth for your children, I think you'll find the Bible emphasizes the former much more than the latter.

Finally, a moral inheritance to your children is valued much more in Scripture than a financial one. Perhaps at some point in the future, we'll be able to dive into this area more fully.

So our two saving principles are as follows:

1. Our present savings should be roughly equivalent to our future needs.
2. It is honoring to God to set aside a portion of your wealth with the express intention of giving it away.

A Biblical View of Hoarding

If the Biblical principle for saving is to match our savings with future expenses reasonably, then it stands to reason that hoarding is excessive saving. It is saving more than we need.

One of the best examples of hoarding as well as one of the stronger teachings against greed is in Luke 12.16-21 (NIV):

And he told them this parable. "The ground of a certain rich man yielded an abundant harvest. He thought to himself, 'What shall I do? I have no place to store my crops.' "Then he said, 'This is what I'll do. I will tear down my barns and build bigger ones, and there I will store my surplus grain. And I'll say to myself, "You have plenty of grain laid up for many years. Take life easy; eat, drink and be merry." ' "But God said to him, 'You fool! This very night your life will be demanded from you. Then who will get what you have prepared for yourself?' "This is how it will be with whoever stores up things for themselves but is not rich toward God."

This is the parable of the rich man who was successful in business and who decided to build bigger barns to hold his increased wealth. He was so successful that he didn't have enough room for all his wealth. So he built larger barns to hold his increase of possessions. Nothing in this story suggests he acquired wealth unethically, illegally, or through oppression.

His actions alone would have revealed what was in his heart. But his words confirmed it: "I'll say to myself, 'You have plenty of good things laid up for many years. Take life easy; eat, drink, and be merry." It was all about him: his money, his wealth, his comfort, his security, and his enjoyment. He had no thought about what God would have him do. He had no thought about giving his wealth away because he had no love for God.

In this parable, the sin of hoarding is about amassing wealth and fortune for ourselves. Hoarding is grounded in believing that our wealth belongs to us, not God. Hoarding does not see wealth as an entrustment from God. Hoarding assumes wealth is not a renewable resource and that economies are a zero-sum game. It is based on the pride of what one has accomplished, bathed in delusion that I did all this on my own, refined in the school of placing my interests ahead of others and expressed through the discontent of always wanting more luxuries in life. Hoarding places one's security for the future in one's money, not God.

Hoarding distorts what a "need" is. I've seen businessmen with a net worth well beyond $30M talk about needing to "add a bit more to their nest egg."

Hoarding creates an insatiable appetite for more and more and more. How much is enough? Always just a bit more.

Hoarding is excessive saving. It is saving more than what you need for future expenses. And know this: **hoarding is lethal to the cause of Christ.**

When we consider our covenant relationship with God, we'll find that hoarding is wholly incompatible. In our covenant relationship with God, we pledge to be faithful to Him. We are loyal to Him. When we hoard, we're faithful to ourselves, not God. We are loyal only to ourselves. In our covenant relationship with God, we love God more than anything or anyone on this earth. When we hoard, we develop a love for our money and what it buys us more than anything else on this earth.

Our covenant relationship with God is characterized by love and loyalty, which flows both ways. When we hoard, we show our love and loyalty to ourselves and our money. When we hoard, we act completely outside our covenant relationship with God. Christ said we'd have to choose: we'll either love money or God, but we can't love both.

The principle we learn is this: *amassing unnecessary wealth for ourselves reveals a love and loyalty for ourselves that is a sin and is a rejection of our covenant relationship with God.*

So, what have we learned this morning?

First, we have learned that taking on debt is the practice of consuming today the fruit of tomorrow's labor. The principle we learned about debt is this:

> *When we borrow, our allegiances become divided between God and our lender. So don't borrow unless God leads you to do so.*

Secondly, when it comes to saving, we learned two principles:
1. *Our present saving should be roughly equivalent to our future need*
2. *It is honoring to God to set aside a portion of your wealth with the express intention of giving it away*

Thirdly, we learned that hoarding is excessive savings. The principle we learned is this: *amassing unnecessary wealth for ourselves reveals a love and loyalty for ourselves and is a rejection of our covenant relationship with God.*

Disciples of Jesus Christ are faithful to God in stewarding all He owns by disadvantaging themselves to advantage His kingdom.

We disadvantage ourselves by purposefully living at a lower standard of living so that we can give more away. Even though we could qualify to take on more debt to live at a higher standard of living, disciples of Jesus Christ reject this notion. Instead, we minimize debt. We reasonably save for the future. And then we give the rest away.

And when we do this, there is a joy and an excitement which is nearly impossible to describe. Borrowing from last week about the paradoxes in Christianity, we will gain by giving. We become rich when we give away our money. We find our lives when we lose them.

So, the stewardship question for us today is this:

Will you intentionally disadvantage yourself in order to advantage the Kingdom of God?

Let's pray.

PART IV

Heart of Stewardship

IN THIS SERIES, we have learned that the Context of Stewardship is our covenant relationship with God. Part of our pledge to be faithful to Him includes being faithful in giving to Him. The Context of Stewardship means that we allow Him to transform our hearts through the supernatural work of the Holy Spirit as He writes His laws into our minds and on our hearts.

We have learned that there are five Foundations of Stewardship:

1. God owns everything
2. God entrusts to us some of that which He owns
3. God Gives Entrustments to Us Based on the Abilities He Has Given to Us
4. Stewards should know their masters well
5. If We Are Faithful to God, We will Reign With Him Throughout Eternity

We have learned that the Life of a Steward means we assume debt only under the direction of the Holy Spirit. We also have learned that we save enough to meet future expenses and then give the rest of our wealth away because amassing wealth for ourselves reveals a love and loyalty to ourselves, not God.

As we have progressed through this series, we've gained more understanding of the central idea of this series:

Disciples of Jesus Christ are faithful to God in stewarding all He owns by disadvantaging themselves to advantage His kingdom.

We become disciples by entering into a covenant relationship with God.

We are faithful to God by entering the new covenant and allowing Him to write His laws into our minds and hearts fully.

We become stewards of all He owns by accepting the Biblical truths of God's ownership of everything and His entrustments to us of that which He owns based on the abilities He has given us.

We disadvantage ourselves by living at a lower standard even though we qualify to take on more debt because we assume debt only when God leads us to do so, and we save for future expenses and give the rest away.

Behind all this is a heart that is warm toward God. As God transforms our hearts, we learn that giving and generosity are heart issues, not ability or capacity issues.

On this final Sunday, we'll look at the Heart of Stewardship. We will look at several key passages and answer what should be the last of our questions or resistances to becoming generous toward God.

So, this morning, I'll walk us through several common questions Christians ask regarding giving. These questions are legitimate, and they need to be answered.

When I run a company, one of my standard operating principles is that no question is out of bounds. If asked with the right attitude, questions can be an important tool in our quiver of learning. So, we'll finish our study of generosity today using a question/answer format this morning.

Does the New Testament Teach that We Must Give to Our Local Church?

The New Testament doesn't directly address giving to a local body, and we're not under the tithe rules anymore since we're not under the Old Testament law. So, I can see how this might be a grey area for Christians. Hence, does God expect me to give to my local church?

Often, we like to have a 1:1:1 relationship when it comes to reading a passage, understanding its meaning and then applying it to our lives. We like it when God is simple and direct with us.

But you'll often find the more important truths of Christianity are taught in multiple passages. God gives us parts of a larger truth spread across the Bible so that we must know His word well to understand His instruction fully.

So we will start in the New Testament and look at several examples of giving to the local church and the ministers who work full time. Then we'll consider one passage from the Old Testament.

In the New Testament, there are four passages I want to draw to your attention:

Philippians 4.15-16 (NIV):

> [15]Moreover, as you Philippians know, in the early days of your acquaintance with the Gospel, when I set out from Macedonia, not one church shared with me in the matter of giving and receiving, except you only; [16]for even when I was in Thessalonica, you sent me aid more than once when I was in need.

Here we see Paul being supported by established churches. He's planting new churches, so those established in their faith in other churches gave to him and his ministries. This passage is also easily applied to supporting missionaries who are called hither and yon to share the Gospel with others.

Galatians 6.6 (NIV):

> Nevertheless, the one who receives instruction in the word should share all good things with their instructor.

Through the ages, scholars have taken this verse to mean that we share our material wealth with those who are in full-time ministry, even though the passage doesn't explicitly say this.

> "Here it lies on the duty of those who are taught to make material provision for their teachers." (1982, A Commentary on the Greek Text—F. F. Bruce)
>
> "If he gives you spiritual things, do not allow him to lack for temporal things." (1870, Charles Spurgeon)
>
> "How disgraceful is it to defraud of their temporal support those by whom our souls are fed—to refuse an earthly recompense to those from whom we receive heavenly benefits! But it is, and always has been, the disposition of the world, freely to bestow on the ministers of Satan every luxury, and hardly to supply godly pastors with necessary food...An earnest desire to preserve a gospel ministry, led to Paul's recommendation that proper attention should be paid to good and faithful pastors." (John Calvin, 1548)

Let's look at another passage: 1 Timothy 5.17-18 (NIV):

> [17]The elders who direct the affairs of the church well are worthy of double honor, especially those whose work is preaching and teaching. [18]For Scripture says, "Do not muzzle an ox while it is treading out the grain," and "The worker deserves his wages."

Again, those who serve us in full-time ministry should be supported by those who associate with that body.

1 Corinthians 9.14 (ESV):

> In the same way, the Lord commanded that those who proclaim the Gospel should get their living by the Gospel.

It makes sense to realize that supporting our local church, under the leadership and direction of our elders, is how we apply these verses to our present day. They're not just descriptive of what took place back then; they are also prescriptive for how we conduct our church affairs today.

The most direct instruction comes from Malachi 3.7-15 (ESV):

> Return to me, and I will return to you, says the Lord of hosts. But you say, 'How shall we return?' [8]Will man rob God? Yet you are robbing me. But you say, 'How have we robbed you?' In your tithes and contributions. [9]You are cursed with a curse, for you are robbing me, the whole nation of you. [10]Bring the full tithe into the storehouse, that there may be food in my house. And thereby put me to the test, says the Lord of hosts, if I will not open the windows of Heaven for you and pour down for you a blessing until there is no more need.

The way to contextualize this Malachi passage for us today is to arrive at the principle that *Christians express their generosity to God by giving financially to their local church so that they can be entrusted by God with more wealth so that they can give more and more away.*

I arrive at this principle based on the following phrases:

- "Bring the full tithe into the storehouse, that there may be food in my house" = give generously to your local church so that your church can nourish members and the surrounding community
- "pour down a blessing" = God will entrust larger sums to us as we prove ourselves faithful in generosity.
- "so there is no more need" = As we give more and more away, we reach a point where our members and community have no more need for our giving.

I can hear you all now: "Wait a minute, Bill. Are you suggesting that God could eradicate all of the social and financial problems in our church and surrounding communities if we just become generous toward God?"

Yep.

Think about it. What would our church be like if we just took this seriously?

- Hunger could be eliminated in our community.

- Poverty could be eradicated in our community.
- Marriages could be saved.
- People would notice that we were living out our faith. They would notice that we were putting our money where our mouth is.
- They would have to admit we took our faith seriously.
- Thousands would come to know God because of our faithfulness in generosity.

They would look at us and say, "I can buy into this,"—"Their faith is real,"—"I want to invest myself in something real and life-changing!"

If you could catch a glimpse of how foundational generosity is to the quality of our faith and the spreading of the Gospel, you'll be forever changed.

So I'll repeat myself here with what I said on the first Sunday:

> *Financial generosity is the solution to so many problems in our church and society that it is difficult to overstate or exaggerate the importance of Christians becoming generous with their money and their wealth.*

But there will be temptations to avoid.

Temptations to Avoid

First, withholding financial giving as a silent protest that you don't like what's happening in your local body is not taught in Scripture. The Scriptures never tell us to withhold our gifts to our local body because we don't like a decision or our personal preferences are unmet. This withholding would be antithetical to our covenant relationship with each other and with God. Stewards don't get a vote in how God spends His money.

Secondly, giving a large gift with the expectation that you'll be honored in the assembly—in other words, giving a gift so that men will praise you—is not taught or supported in Scripture. Christ taught in Matthew 6 that our giving should be in secret. And by the way, know that the pastors here never know who gives how much. Only two people know this on our staff. Our pastors and elders never know who is giving how much to this church.

Thirdly, treating your giving as a form of financial investing in which you give to God with the expectation that He will give back to you more than you gave so that you can spend more on yourself is essentially what the prosperity Gospel is. It is a corrupted, ungodly theology.

So, to summarize, we've learned one principle thus far:

> *Christians express their generosity to God by giving financially to their local church so that they can be entrusted by God with more wealth so that they can give more and more away.*

So, are each of us required to give to our local church? The answer is "yes".

What if I don't Have Enough Money to Give and How Much Should I Give?

This question is hard in one sense because I will use a parable about a poor widow. But our church is located in Maple Grove, MN, in 2021—hardly a poor community. Based on the census numbers, we're the 1,538th richest community in the United States out of ~27,000 communities. Our median household income is $125K. Maple Grove is in the top 5.5% of the most affluent communities in the most affluent generation in the most affluent country this world has ever seen.

Now, we pull from surrounding communities as well. We pull from a radius of about 14-15 miles, and there is variation in the median income across these communities. But our church is located in Maple Grove.

So, while we might "feel" poor at times, we still live at standards and with conveniences unthinkable by most people who have walked the face of this earth.

Happily, the Scriptures address both amount and ability. Let's read Luke 21.1-4 (NIV):

[1]As Jesus looked up, he saw the rich putting their gifts into the temple treasury. [2]He also saw a poor widow put in two very small copper coins. [3]"Truly I tell you," he said, "this poor widow has put in more than all the others. [4]All these people gave their gifts out of their wealth; but she out of her poverty put in all she had to live on."

This parable shows a poor widow—so poor that her wealth consisted of two copper coins. In today's dollars, the value of these coins is debated, with conclusions ranging from fractions of a penny to nearly a dollar per coin. So, if we take the highest value, the widow gave two dollars to her local synagogue.

Her example teaches us that even the smallest amounts given to God are important because they reflect a heart that wants to give to Him. She could have easily said something like this: "I'm poor, I have nothing to live on, so I can't afford to give to God."

But this wasn't her attitude. She wanted to give to God. She wanted to be generous. And she acted aligned with what was in her heart—she gave all she had to live on because she had already given her whole heart to God. She intentionally disadvantaged herself to advantage God's kingdom.

Those who are generous toward God will always have money to give to God. Those not generous toward Him will never have enough money to give to God, even if they earn millions yearly. Generosity is never about ability. It is always about one's heart.

Sacrificing for someone else—disadvantaging ourselves for someone else—is always a heart issue. This is why parents often sacrifice for their children. They sacrifice because they love their children.

Show me someone who won't sacrifice for God, and I'll show you someone who doesn't love God. Show me someone who won't sacrifice for their local body, and I'll show you someone who doesn't love their local body.

Christ mentioned sacrificial giving in John 15.13(NIV):

Greater love has no one than this: to lay down one's life for one's friends.

The Apostle John wrote this in 1 John 3.16(NIV):

> This is how we know what love is: Jesus Christ laid down his life for us. And we ought to lay down our lives for our brothers and sisters.

The principle we learn is this: *When we love, we sacrifice.*

When we apply this to financial generosity, it means we give sacrificially. We don't give only out of our abundance. We give sacrificially. We disadvantage ourselves in order to advantage others.

This means that even the poorest of the poor can give something to God. Even if it is only $1/month, we sacrifice that to God.

Sacrifice is another paradox in Christianity. Christ said in Matthew 16.25-26 (ESV):

> For whoever wants to save his life will lose it, but whoever loses his life for me will find it. What good will it be for a man if he gains the whole world, but loses his own soul?

What does losing your life look like? For some, like missionary Jim Elliot, it means martyrdom. But many of us "lose our lives" daily. We sacrifice our time and talent, subjecting our vocations to Jesus' imperatives. We sacrifice the right to enjoy money and possessions any way we please. We are called to sacrifice to Christ's lordship our very thoughts and desires, our fears and our foibles, and let Him transform us into His image. We must be willing to sacrifice anything we value as essential to "life" as we know it. Discipleship and stewardship in the kingdom require total allegiance. It's a steep price to pay, but it's a great deal with eternity in the balance. As Jim Elliot wrote in his journal: "he is no fool who gives what he cannot keep to gain that which he cannot lose."

The world system aims at fairness and equal rights and what is required of us. It asks What must I do? The Kingdom of God aims at sacrifice and giving up our rights and asks, How can I sacrifice for God and others? Sacrifice is what Paul meant when he wrote this in Philippians 3.7-8 (ESV):

^{7}But whatever gain I had, I counted as loss for the sake of Christ. ^{8}Indeed, I count everything as loss because of the surpassing worth of knowing Christ Jesus my Lord. For his sake I have suffered the loss of all things and count them as rubbish, in order that I may gain Christ.

So, two more questions: what if you don't have enough money to give and how much should you give? I think the answer is more about your heart. Do you want to give? Do you want to be generous? Have you allowed God to transform your heart so you are eager to give sacrificially? If you're not willing to give sacrificially, are you willing to be made willing?

God should direct the precise amount which you give. It is important that, as a steward, you give the amounts as God directs you to give and trust Him to meet your needs. When we obey God, He is responsible for protecting and providing for us. When we disobey God by not giving as He directs, we get outside His protection and provision. Giving is a heart issue. It is a covenant issue. It is a trust issue. It is a stewardship issue. It is never about amount, ability or capacity. Give as God directs, save as God directs and trust His protection and provision for your future.

Now, there is false teaching to avoid, and it is this: any teaching about trading time and talent for financial giving is not Biblical. Nowhere in the Bible do we find God approving of us not giving financially and replacing financial giving with giving an in-kind gift of time or talent. Nowhere in the Bible do we see believers not being generous while serving God more and more. Any teaching that one can withhold financial giving to God and yet work more to make up for the difference is unbiblical. Such a tradeoff decision is never taught in the Scriptures.

So, are we required to give to our local church? The answer is Yes.

What if I don't have enough money to give? Well, if your heart is generous, you'll give out of that heart—even if it is only two copper coins.

So, how much should I give? The precise amounts will differ for each person, but you should give the amounts God directs you to. Percentages here don't matter. Some will barely be able to give 1%. Others should give 80% or 90%. The point is to give sacrificially in the amounts directed by God.

What about Giving to Other Ministries Beside My Church?

When God directs our giving, from time to time, He may direct us to give to other ministries besides our local church. For example, in addition to giving at *The Grove*, Kathy and I support children in Haiti through the Global Fingerprints program. And we support Open Doors, a ministry to persecuted Christians worldwide. We often refer to these ministries as *para-church* organizations. Much of our missionary support goes through organizations like the Free church or Cru or Navigators.

The concept of para-church organizations, as we have them today, doesn't exist in the Bible. So, a principle I use in the application of Scripture, which we discussed last week, is this: emphasize what the Bible emphasizes and rely on God's voice to direct my steps in those areas where the Scriptures are silent.

In brief, as God directs, we give to these other organizations.

But we are never taught in the Bible that we can trade off our giving to the local church to give to para-church organizations. The Bible is clear that directing our giving to our local body is our first priority.

I want to talk to business owners for just a moment. Because the Bible has no concept of corporations, any notion that your corporation should tithe as well as you personally is a decision to be directed by God. There's no prohibition to a business tithing. But there's also no Biblical mandate for a business to tithe either. So ask the Lord and follow His direction.

What Have we learned today?

We have learned two basic principles:

> *Christians express their generosity to God by giving financially to their local church so that they can be entrusted by God with more wealth so that they can give more and more away.*

> *When we love, we sacrifice.*

So our stewardship question to consider is this:

If you love this local body, the Grove, will you commit to sacrificial financial giving to this body?

At the beginning of this series, I mentioned that I assumed what I would teach would be new information for many in this church.

But now, everyone here has the same light in which to walk. Everyone here now has a choice: either we'll joyfully obey the light we have been given and grow in our maturity with God, or we'll resist this teaching from God. Either we'll choose to enter the great life of generosity God offers us or settle for the American life of debt, hoarding and amassing wealth for ourselves.

We become rich when we become poor. We become strong when we become weak. We find our life by losing it. We lay up for ourselves treasures in Heaven when we sacrifice our treasures on this earth. We give away what we cannot keep to gain what we cannot lose. We disadvantage ourselves so that we can intentionally advantage God's kingdom. And when we disadvantage ourselves, we find a life more full of joy than we ever thought possible. When we hunger and thirst for God, we will be satisfied. And it's just a foretaste of what Heaven will be like.

Will you participate in the new covenant by allowing God to write His laws into your *mind and heart?*

Will you be a faithful steward who properly cares for God's entrustments and takes the time and effort to know Him intimately?

Will you intentionally disadvantage yourself in order to advantage the Kingdom of God?

If you love this local body, the Grove, will you commit to sacrificial financial giving to this body?

After receiving this teaching from God's holy word, I pray that we will each willingly and joyfully commit our hearts and minds to God and become more generous toward Him and draw closer to him than we ever thought possible.

Let's Pray.

More Books By Bill English

A Christian Theology of Business Ownership: An Introduction for Christian Entrepreneurs on What the Bible Says About Owning a Business.

Biblical Wisdom for Business Leaders: Thirty Sayings from Proverbs.

What the Bible Has to Say About Owning a Business: An Abridged Version of "A Christian Theology of Business Ownership."

Working for a Difficult Boss: Lessons from the Life of Daniel

All books can be found at bibleandbusiness.com and are sold through Amazon and other online book retailers.

Connect Through Social Media

You can connect with Bill through social media and other means:
Email: bill@bibleandbusness.com
Twitter: @biblebusiness
Facebook Page: www.facebook.com/bibleandbusiness
Facebook discussion: www.facebook.com/groups/bibleandbusiness
Instagram: www.instagram.com/Biblebusiness
Linkedin: www.linkedin.com/company/9189201
Website: www.bibleandbusiness.com
Youtube: www.youtube.com/c/bibleandbusiness

About Bill English

Bill English is an entrepreneur, author, speaker, and business advisor. With decades of experience, he has assisted other business owners, led a national training company, served as an interim CEO for two other companies, and is currently the CEO of a 20M+ healthcare business.

Bill holds two master's degrees—one in divinity and the other in counseling psychology—both from Trinity Evangelical Divinity School.

Bill has written fourteen technical books. His most recent book is Working for a Difficult Boss: Lessons from the Life of Daniel. This book was written for mid- and upper-level managers in for-profit companies who must be faithful to God while managing down, out, and up. Bill has also written Biblical Wisdom for Business Leaders: Thirty Sayings from Proverbs, a book for Christian business leaders. He has also authored A Christian Theology of Business Ownership: An Introduction for Christian Entrepreneurs on What the Bible Says About Owning a Business and "thinks out loud" at bibleandbusiness.com.

He has been married to Kathy for twenty-eight years, and they live in Minneapolis, Minnesota, where summer is the best eleven days of the year!

www.ingramcontent.com/pod-product-compliance
Lightning Source LLC
Chambersburg PA
CBHW071850020426
42331CB00007B/1938